HOW I GOT MILLIONAIRE MENTALITY

Bill Swad, Sr.

*This book is dedidcated to
my precious wife Sally.*

ISBN 0-939241-78-1

Bill Swad, Sr.
c/o Christian Center
298 South Rocky Fork Drive
Gahanna, Ohio 43230

INTRODUCTION

This book is not about a boy raised in poverty in eastern Ohio — nor the story of a man who became the wealthy owner of some of America's largest automobile dealerships. It is about the dramatic transformation of a heart, soul, and mind from the syndrome of doubt and failure to *Millionaire Mentality*.

During the past thirty years I have counseled with hundreds of people who have been trapped by self-doubt, unbelief, and fear. Many have asked, "Bill, what's your secret?" Or, "How can I know success?"

In the pages that follow, you will discover much more than what happened to Bill Swad, Sr. You'll learn sound, solid principles that will allow you to fulfill God's greatest expectations for your life.

The questions we'll answer include

— What is the secret of total commitment?
— Can a person be truly "reprogrammed" for achievement?"
— How can you have a transformed mind?
— How should money be perceived?
— What about the wealth of a sinner?
— Is the "Prosperity Gospel" a great danger?
— What about "giving and getting?"
— Is there a link between tithing and success?
— What are the three reasons for failure?
— How do the laws of God, man, and nature differ?
— Is *extra*-ordinary personal achievement truly possible for you?

Plus much more.

Begin immediately to apply these principles and precepts to your life. The dream of your future — often an elusive and ambiguous goal — is closer than you ever imagined.

After decades of applying the power of God-given *Millionaire Mentality,* I am excited to share this volume with you.

CONTENTS

1

THE DREAM THAT ALMOST DIED

It seemed like an impossible dream! But the headline on a feature in the Columbus (Ohio) Dispatch told the story:

"From Three Cars to Five Dealerships."

How could a boy raised in the poverty of the Great Depression build one of the largest automotive empires east of the Mississippi River and become a multimillionaire? Annual sales had topped $400 million. I had to pinch myself to realize the story was about *me* — Bill Swad.

This book contains the story of a great transformation. It is the account of how I discarded a deeply rooted poverty perspective and discovered *Millionaire Mentality*. But what is most important is that the same thing can happen to you. I believe you have the potential to fulfill God's dream for your life.

As you read what I am about to share, I firmly feel you are going to be inspired to say, "That's it!" Instantly, you will focus on the great idea God has for your future.

There have been times in my life when the Lord has flooded me with a great burst of imagination and creativity. I believe you are about to experience the same thing.

"Millionaire Mentality" will be more than a glib phrase; it will become your mind-set, your lifestyle — as natural as breathing.

I was born in Martins Ferry with a failure mentality — and even worse. That is the little town in eastern Ohio where my father, an immigrant from Syria, tried to scratch out a living. There were eight of us living in half of a house at 1311 Zane Highway — mom, dad, and six kids. I was the youngest. My father spoke only broken English and we were teased and called "hunkeys" by the townspeople.

For me, prosperity meant that I had a nickel. With that I could walk down to Mr. Chick's store and get a candy bar or an ice cream cone.

When I was five I would sit on the front porch with my older brother Ken, and watch the cars go by. I was fascinated with them. We would try to name every one — a Ford, a Chevy, a Graham-Paige, a Willys Knight, or whatever. Then we would try to guess the year of the car.

"Some day I am going to have a car like that," I told my brother — never dreaming that I would own acres and acres of them.

I really didn't know how poor we were — I thought everybody lived like the Swads. Oh, there was one fellow I knew as a kid that made it to the bigtime. Lou Groza became a football hero with the Cleveland Browns. But that was about it.

"Depression Soles"

"Don't throw away the Shredded Wheat box." I can still hear my mother's voice when I was about six years old. The stiff cardboard dividers in the box became the inside liners for our shoes. Then, mother would spend about 20 cents for what were called "depression soles," — an outer layer that was glued to the bottom of the shoe.

Actually, I felt fortunate. Some of the kids in first grade at South School had no shoes at all.

My uncle moved to Phoenix, Arizona, when I was about nine years old. I can still remember the picture he sent us of his house. In the photo was a big palm tree growing in his yard. I studied that picture again and again and never forgot the image.

Had you told me as a child that I would someday have a luxury home on a private golf course in Boca Raton, Florida, with a huge canary palm tree in my backyard, I would have said, "You're crazy!" It just was not possible.

I grew up with a failure mentality. It faced me at every turn and became the only reality I knew.

We moved from place to place, seeking a better life. To Cadiz Pike, then over to Uhrichsville, then up to a farmhouse on a hill near Gilmore, Ohio. Many people called it "Killmore" because there were so many murders in the area.

Life on the farm taught me what hard work was all about. It was tough. To make some extra money I'd work at a neighbor's farm hoeing corn in the burning sun for $1 a day. How else could I buy some gas for my 20-year-old car?

Life at home was not a rose garden. My father was an alcoholic whose drinking binges made us all shudder. Repeatedly, he became so violent that those who knew him kept their distance. I feared for my young life when I smashed the family tractor during World

War II. Surviving the accident was easy compared to the wrath I would face from dad. But somehow I lived through it.

I was just 19 years old when my father died. His casket was placed in the living room of our old house and people came from miles around for the burial. He had just bought the farm and had financed 100% of the selling price. Though I was the youngest, somehow the responsibility for the mortgage fell on my shoulders. Ready or not, I became a man in a hurry.

After finding a buyer to bail us out of the farm, I found some land with two small houses on it in Licking County, near Columbus. A wonderful man, Ellis T. Reese, trusted me enough to provide the financing. It was far from a mansion, but we were proud to call it our home.

Part-Time Entrepreneur

From job to job, I did whatever it took to survive — including milking 48 Holsteins twice a day at the Valley View Dairy Farm.

After moving to Columbus, I found work at North American Aviation in 1952 for $1.47 an hour. It certainly was not the job of my dreams, but it put food on the table.

My fascination with cars had not diminished. In fact, during my very first year at the aircraft plant, I decided to become a part-time entrepreneur — and I didn't even know what the word meant. For some reason I got the

11

idea that I could buy an old car, fix it up, and perhaps sell it for a little profit. I found an empty lot over on Main Street and rented it for $25 a month. It seemed like $1000 at the time.

The sign on the lot read:

"Bill's Used Cars."

Working the night shift, every evening during my meal break I would run over to see if anyone was interested in the one or two clunkers I was trying to sell.

With some used lumber I bought from North American, a friend helped me build a little six-foot-square office on the lot. Sales were not spectacular, but I averaged selling one car every week at a profit of about $175. Big money in 1952 — much more than I was making at the plant.

After running the part-time car lot for nearly a year, my boss at the plant walked up and made me a proposition. "Bill, if you will close that dumb side business you have, I'll give you all the over-time you want."

I did not know what it meant to have someone steal your dream, but it was happening to me.

"You can make time-and-a-half and even some double time," the foreman promised.

It was perhaps the most stupid move of my life, but I listened to the man and closed my little business. For the next three years I gave my energy to the aircraft plant, but deep inside, the vision of being my own boss kept gnawing at me.

The promise of over-time sounded good when it was made, but the extra work was not always available. By 1956 I had three jobs — at the aircraft plant, selling gloves for my brother Ernie, and part time as a car salesman at the local Ford dealership. I hardly had time to breathe — and the sad part was that for all my effort, I was making very little money.

The car business became so good for me that in late 1956 I quit my job at North American and began selling Fords full time.

Some Fatherly Advice

One day, when the showroom was empty, I was sitting on the edge of a desk, talking with one of the older salesmen. I told him about the little used car lot I started in 1952. "What happened? " he asked.

When I shared the story of how I gave it up because of the promises of my foreman, he gave me some fatherly advice. "You know, Bill, you ought to start another used car business right now. Because if you don't, you're liable to be sitting here on this desk selling these Fords for the next 20 years. And you'll always wonder why you didn't become your own boss."

I took his advice.

"Sir, I need to borrow $1000 to finance the inventory of a new business I am starting." That's what I told the manager of the Economy Loan Company.

"What kind of a business?" he asked.

"Used cars. And with the $1000 I am going to buy three vehicles."

I told him of my earlier car business and he decided to take a chance.

At 8:00 a.m., on the morning of April 8, 1957, I arrived at my new place of business. It was a lot near the corner of Hamilton Road and Broad Street in Columbus. The rent was $75 a month. I hung a string of six lightbulbs and posted a sign that read:

"BILL SWAD MOTOR SALES."

Walking past the three old cars I had financed, I opened the door to the little sales building in the center of the lot. The business would not open until 9:00 a.m., but I arrived an hour early to spend time with my business partner. His name was Jesus.

"Ready for Business"

I was the least likely candidate to form a partnership with Christ. In my early years, the church we attended was not truly a church at all. The leader was an avowed atheist and — looking back — I was nothing more than an agnostic. My knowledge of Scripture was zero and that is what my life reflected.

From the age of 14, drinking had become my preoccupation. By the time I was 21 I was a chronic alcoholic, drinking a fifth and a half of whiskey every day. I was also a three-pack-a-day smoker from the time I was 15.

For Bill Swad, life was tough and I was going to kick my way through it. It was after my marriage at the age of 20 and the birth of our first son, that I came face to face with the reality of a power that was greater than I had ever imagined. Our son, Bill, Jr., was just six weeks old when he became deathly ill. The doctor told us that his severely infected hernia had become life-threatening.

At almost the same time, God, in His mercy, sent to our home a young couple who were attending a pentecostal Bible school. They presented the simple Plan of Salvation.

Later that night, alone, upstairs in that little farm house, I had a "Damascus Road" experience. At 4:40 a.m., December 23, 1951, the scales of skepticism and unbelief fell from my eyes. From the depths of my heart, I cried,

"Jesus, forgive me of my sin. I am asking you to be the Lord of my life!"

From that moment, I began to absorb the Word of God like a sponge. As a child in Martins Ferry I had no idea that there was a revolutionary book written

15

called the Bible. I was ignorant of the fact that the Word was filled with principles that can lead a person out of poverty.

Now, in that little sales office on Hamilton Road I got down on my knees and said, "Lord, this is your business. I totally dedicate it to you. Everything I do from this moment on is for your glory and honor." As I continued to pray, I felt the Lord Himself enter that little building and lay His hand on my life. We have been partners ever since.

I looked at my watch. It was exactly 9:00 a.m.

Bill Swad Motor Sales was open for business.

2

A GREEN CADILLAC

At about three minutes after nine, April 8, 1957, I got excited when I saw what appeared to be my first customer. But it was just the mailman.

He handed me some junk mail labeled "Occupant," and said, "Mister, what are you planning to do out here?"

"Well, what does it look like to you?" I responded.

I had a little sign that I paid $5 for that said, "BILL SWAD MOTOR SALES." The used desk and chair were only $15. And there were three cars on the lot. I would have had more, but $1000 was all I could borrow.

The mailman said, "It looks like you're trying to start a used car business."

I laughed a little and replied, "I'm not *trying* to do anything. I *have* started a used car lot — and I've dedicated it to God. In fact, I just finished talking with the Lord and He said it's going to prosper tremendously!"

His face became very serious as he said, "Let me tell you something, young man. I've been carrying the mail out here for a long, long time and there have been a number of little businesses started on this corner. But every single one of them has been a failure. Every one!"

If that was supposed to scare me, it didn't work. You see, I had just finished talking with my Father and I was filled with His power and joy.

I had only been a Christian for six years, but that morning I felt like Joshua as I walked around that lot and prayed. I didn't want the walls to fall down — I was just claiming God's blessing on my business.

The mailman just shook his head as he left and reminded me,

"Don't forget what I told you about this corner. I think it's kind of jinxed."

"Jinxed?" I thought. "He doesn't know the God I

18

serve."

Not ten minutes later I heard the sound of a car driving on the lot. By 9:30 that morning I sold the first car.

"Hallelujah!" I thought. "We're on our way."

There I was, on a little two-lane road with a big corn field behind me. I soon heard what the car dealers in town were saying:

"That Holy Roller out there is going to starve to death in the mud."

There wasn't any black top on my lot, just a ton of mud and a little gravel.

I certainly did not mind being called a Holy Roller. At least I wasn't the kind that woke up Sunday morning and rolled over to get some more sleep.

Within two years, their tune began to change. We had become the largest used car dealer in the state of Ohio.

How did it happen? I began to believe what God's Word said. I knew that absolutely nothing was impossible. My mentality was transformed from fear to faith.

"I have so many problems," a friend once told me.

"That's funny," I responded. "I have so many opportunities!"

We were both talking about the same thing. If you

put obstacles in "work clothes," they become openings for success.

Here's how it worked in my business.

The "Interceptor"

In 1959, the State Highway Patrol cars used on the Ohio Turnpike were leased from Spitzer Brothers — one of the largest new car dealerships in the state. For some reason the government agency canceled the leases and the company was stuck with a large quantity of cars. Even worse, they were about to lose a considerable amount of money.

I hadn't been in business too long, but I received a phone call from a friend in Cleveland. He said, "Bill, the Spitzer's have nearly 200 of these Highway Patrol cars. I think you ought buy a few and see if you can turn them on your lot."

Immediately I went to Cleveland and drove one back. The minute I drove it on my lot, someone found out that it had a souped up "interceptor" engine and he bought it on the spot. "This thing will fly without wings," he said.

On Monday morning people were driving to my lot asking, "Do you have any more of those special Highway Patrol cars?" Evidently the customer took the vehicle to a local drag strip and the word spread like wildfire.

I called a friend at a local bank I'd been doing some business with and said, "Wade, let me tell you about some patrol cars with interceptor engines I can get up in Cleveland." He advanced me enough to haul ten of them back to Columbus.

All ten were gone within a few days and I was back for more. Financially, it was a bonanza unlike anything I had experienced. On the sale of an average used car, my profit at that time was between $150 and $300, but on these special buys I was clearing over $1000 each.

I wound up buying nearly all of the patrol cars. You don't have to be a genius at math to know that the Lord was blessing me.

What was a problem for a major car dealership became an opportunity for me

— and I solved their dilemma in the process. There was another bonus. The Spitzer family became respected friends and attended meetings where I gave my personal testimony. And I had the honor of praying with them.

One of the commitments I made to the Lord when I started my business was that I would never miss an opportunity to present Christ — even if it meant that I might lose a deal. Winning souls was more important than winning sales.

21

Splurging on a Sedan DeVille

"Bill, we're having a big convention of the Full Gospel Business Men's Fellowship International at the Americana Hotel in Miami Beach. Can you come down and be one of our speakers?" The call was from Demos Shakarian, president of the organization. It was July, 1960. (Not only did I address the convention, but was elected as one of the International Directors of FGBMFI.)

Calls like that became more frequent as the word spread that there was an excited, Spirit-filled automobile dealer in Columbus that just couldn't stop talking about Jesus.

I accepted the invitation and immediately began to look around for the best car I could find to make the trip. I splurged and bought a Cadillac that was almost new — it was the best car I had ever purchased. Actually, I put too much money in it, but after my success with the sale of the Highway Patrol cars I rationalized that I deserved it. It was a green four-door Sedan DeVille.

When I returned from the Florida trip I immediately put the car on my lot. The way I figured it, the money from that car could buy ten smaller ones. And if I got the right deals, I might make a whopping $500 on each car — $ 5,000 profit.

You may find it hard to believe, but I have always been a fiscal conservative — never spending more than

22

I made. I realized from the start that plowing profits back into increased inventory was the only way to grow. Any other route is a sure-fire boulevard to bankruptcy.

After being in the business three years, I had a reputation for selling clean, quality economy cars the average person could afford to buy. Not junkers, just nice used cars. So having a rather new cadillac on the lot was a novelty.

The advertisement in the local paper read:

"1960 Sedan DeVille, Green 4-door. Like new. Less than 10,000 miles."

I was anxious to unload it since it had tied up my money.

The ad ran several times and each day I prayed, "Now Lord, you know I really need a buyer for this car."

It was late on a Saturday evening. My two sales-men had left for the day and I stayed open waiting for just one more customer. As it is for so many business-es, just one extra sale can keep the operation in the black.

"How Late Are You Open?"

"Hello. Are you the people with the ad in today's

paper on the '60 Cadillac?" said a booming voice on the phone.

"Yes, sir. You've reached the right place," I responded.

"Is it really as nice as the description?"

"Just like new," I told him. "I bought it for myself, drove it to Florida and back and I just want to sell it."

The voice on the other end asked, "How late are you open?"

"How late do you want me to be open?" I chuckled.

He said, "Well, we are downtown Columbus and we've looked all day for a 4-door Cadillac and we can't find one that's decent. We want to look at yours on our way back to Chillicothe." The town was about 60 miles south of Columbus. "We'll be there in about half an hour."

"Yes sir. I'll be here!"

I jumped out the door of my little office and made sure the Cadillac was just perfect. After a light dusting with the polishing cloth I parked it in the brightest spot on the gravel lot. (By now I had 15 bulbs on my string of lights.)

The minute those two fellows got out of their car I knew they were buyers. If you have ever been in the car business you can spot a buyer from a shopper in half a second. I thought, "No question about it, these are motivated buyers." It was late — they were tired

— they wanted the car and liked it. Like a fisherman, I knew I had them on the hook. I could "smell" the deal.

The guys took a little ride while I was pacing and praying at the lot. When they came back, the driver jumped out and said, "I'll take it."

As we walked into the tiny salesroom, I could not avoid hearing their constant foul-mouthed language. A few years earlier I would never have noticed — and probably would have joined right in. But when the Lord cleaned me up, he also reprogrammed my vocabulary.

If you have ever been a smoker — and have quit — you detest the smell of smoke. The same thing is true of a former drinker. Having been an alcoholic, I can't stand to be around a drunk. It reminds me of the past.

I did my best to ignore their cursing so I could finish the paperwork and get them on their way. But the voice of the Holy Spirit kept whispering,

"Don't forget your commitment. Tell them about Jesus. Tell them about Jesus. "

As I was writing up the deal, the buyer told me the name of his banker and said, "You can call him right now and you'll have your check first thing Monday morning."

Believe me, those were the best words I had heard all week. I thought, "Great day, I'll have my money in just two days." I really needed it at that particular time.

"You Must Be Crazy!"

The next words coming out of my lips I could hardly believe. I laid my pencil down on the desk and said, "You guys don't need this Cadillac. You need Jesus!"

They looked at me in total disbelief. The buyer was the manager of a radio station, and with him was a young fellow with a very deep voice who was the newscaster at the station.

The manager said, "You must be crazy!"

I said, "That's right. I am. I'm crazy about Jesus! And I want to tell you about Him because He will change your life."

After listening for about 10 minutes as I told them how the Lord had completely transformed me, they interrupted and said,

"Hey, look. We didn't come here to get preached at — we came to buy a Cadillac. Now are you going to sell us the car or not?"

I shook my head and said, "Nope. I'm not going to sell you the car until you accept Jesus." I had never spoken with such authority and boldness in my life.

Was I worried about the sale? Not any more. Because I knew God was my source — I knew it then and I know it now. The thought of seeing that sale fly out that window never bothered me because I knew God owned the cattle on a thousand hills — and the hills, too.

"I'll make a deal with you," the station manager calmly said. "Whatever you want me to do about Jesus, I'll do it. But not at this moment. You see, I need this car right now and have to have it for Monday." He told me it was important that he be able to drive it home that very night. "This Jesus thing can wait until next week."

"What day?" I asked him.

"Wednesday," he said nervously.

"All right. What time?"

He said, "You name it."

I said, "I'll be at your house in Chillicothe at seven o'clock sharp."

The man promised to invite a few of his neighbors. "We'll set up some chairs in my basement and have some refreshments and you can come and tell us about Jesus."

"Fine," I said. "I'll be there."

I wondered if he would remember, and he probably wondered if I would show up. But when I walked into his basement that Wednesday night I was shocked to see over 20 people packed into that room — his friends and neighbors.

For more than an hour I told them about the Lord and shared my testimony of how I was converted through the miracle healing of our infant son. And as I prayed, it seemed that every person in the room accepted Christ as their Savior.

You may ask, "What happened to those two men who bought my Sedan DeVille? The cursing station manager, Ray Anderson, became an ordained minister of the Church of God (Cleveland, Tennessee), and has pastored several churches. And the young announcer, Steven B. Stevens, became the head of one of the nation's largest Shakley distributorships, the voice of "The Bible on Tape," and an "Ambassador at Large" for Christ.

What's so important about a green Cadillac? Not a thing. By now it is rusting in a junk yard. But the hearts that were changed in Chillicothe continue to give life to a hurting world.

3

"BOLD AS A LION"

Is there hope for the hopeless?

If you had asked me that question during the first twenty-one years of my life, I would have said, "No!"

But now I am teaching people about God's principles of prosperity — and how to cultivate the seeds of greatness the Lord has placed within every person. More than once I have seen a weak, timid loser become as bold as a lion.

You say, "Bill, it's easy for you to talk about success. You've got it made. You're already a winner."

Please understand that I didn't learn God's laws of

blessing *after* I had built a thriving business. As a young man I had no idea that God was on my side, that He loved me, and wanted to help me. But the moment I gave Him my life, I became totally absorbed in the Word — and listened intently to the men and women of God that gave me instruction.

It was only after a total immersion in the things of the Lord that I was able to apply His Word to my business.

It Was Revolutionary

My friend, you will get out of life exactly what you expect. If you envision the future on the garbage dump of life, that is the filth in which you will live. How do you think I became a drunken bum at the age of twenty-one?

Coming face to face with Christ, however, changed all that.

I was like a wide-eyed child when I began to read what God had planned for my life. I'll never forget the first time I read the scripture: "The thief does not come except to steal, and to kill, and to destroy. I have come that they may have life, and that they may have it more abundantly." (John 10:10)

That verse was revolutionary to me.

By the time I started my business in 1957, the Word had become such a part of my daily life that I woke up every morning expecting that something good was going to happen to me.

For many, however, the seeds of greatness are constantly being choked by the weeds of fear. They don't know that the Apostle Paul said, "For God has not given us a spirit of fear, but of power and of love and of a sound mind." (2 Timothy 1:7)

The seeds God has planted in your life are not there by accident. They are an important part of His great plan for your future.

I didn't fully comprehend that in 1952 when I allowed the foreman at the aircraft plant to steal my dream.

But by 1957, when the mailman tried to sow seeds of doubt by telling me that every business had failed at my new location, I laughed at his seeds of fear and would not allow them to take root.

At one time I worried about going broke. But then God gave me a wonderful revelation: *I did not have to worry about going broke because I was already broke.* I had been broke all of my life, so what was the difference? What became much more important was being *broken* before the Lord — to allow Him to form and shape my life in His image.

Today, when I sense that fear is about to knock, I let faith answer the door. Here is what Scripture tells me: "The wicked flee when no one pursues, but the righteous are bold as a lion." (Proverbs 28:1) And Jesus said, "Let not your heart be troubled, neither let it be afraid." (John 14:27)

When a contractor begins to build an office building or a new house, he digs a trench and fills it with cement — it's called a "footer." That is what provides the foundation and strength for the walls and vertical posts.

The "footings" I lacked as a child became mine as I began to open the Word. It caused my faith to become "rock solid" through every wind and storm.

It also gave me the boldness and confidence to accept great opportunities and challenges.

"Smiling Phil From Mullica Hill"

Early in 1962 I was called by a group of businessmen to speak at a youth conference in New Jersey. At the same gathering was a successful American Motors dealer by the name of Phil Gardner. He was known by his media advertising as "Smiling Phil from Mullica Hill."

After the meeting he walked up to me and said, "Bill, you ought to be an American Motors dealer."

"I'd really like to," I told him. "I've been trying to get the franchise, but the district manager told me, 'Absolutely never. No dice.'"

My used car business had grown to the point that I felt I was ready to get into the new car business, but the right opportunity didn't seem to exist.

Phil said, "Don't worry too much about the district manager. I know the president of AMC, Roy Abernathy. I'll contact him and tell him to give you a call. He'll give you a franchise — I'm telling you, you'll get it."

Smiling Phil was as good as his word. The next week I answered the phone and a voice said, "This is Roy Abernathy." Within a few weeks I had the franchise, built a building, and was off and running with my first new car dealership.

Within three years we became the largest AMC dealer in the world.

Then we added a Chrysler-Plymouth dealership and became one of the top four in the country. Next it was a large Lincoln-Mercury dealership, then Datsun, Chevrolet, and a "quad point" in northern Ohio where I had franchises for Pontiac, Buick, Cadillac, and GMC Truck.

Not every car model was a winner. But somehow we turned the sour lemons into splendid lemonade.

"They're Bombs"

Do you remember the Marlin? American Motors spent a fortune on a car that looked more like a fish — so it was aptly named. When it was introduced, I told Roy Abernathy it wouldn't fly, but they had invested millions in the model and it was too late to pull back. The three cars we had seemed to sit on our sales lot forever.

Then one Saturday the zone manager called and said, "Bill, I've got a hugh stock of Marlins piled up and I've got to get rid of them — or they're going to get rid of me. Can you help?"

"I've had three of those crazy things for over a year. They're bombs," I told him.

"Bill, I've got over 100 of them on one lot. How many can you take? I have talked to every dealer in the state and since you're the biggest in the country I figured you'd know how to move them."

Having three you couldn't get rid of was like having the plague. They were good cars, but over-priced and under-styled.

I wasn't excited about the prospect of a deal, but in a few minutes he phoned back and said, "Bill, I've called Detroit and if you'll take all of them, we can let you have the cars at less than half of what they actually cost." Not only that, but he promised to deliver them freight-free.

"How many?" I asked.

"We found a few more. There's a couple hundred

34

of them."

"Two hundred cars?" I questioned. "Where on earth am I going to put them?"

"No problem. We'll bring them to you 30 at a time."

I thought for a second about what Jesus said: "With men this is impossible, but with God all things are possible." (Matthew 19:26)

As those Marlin's began rolling off the trucks, I thought, "We'd better have one whale of a sale."

The full page advertisement we ran said:

MARLIN HEADQUARTERS
OF THE U.S.A.
I bought them all!
Come and get them!
They won't last long!
I bought them cheap!
You can buy them cheap!

The response to the ad was unbelievable. We had a riot — people were almost fighting over them. I had Marlins all up and down Hamilton Road. It seemed like everybody I knew bought one of those things.

"Faith 101"

The word spread about what happened at our AMC

dealership, and a few weeks later I had a call from the Chrysler zone manager that the company was going to stop importing Simcas. It was a little three-cylinder import.

"We've got about 125 at the port of Baltimore we've got to unload fast," he told me. "I'll make you a deal you can't refuse."

There were four Chrysler dealers in the metropolitan area and between us we had five Simcas — and some had been on the lot for two years. But, remembering what happened with the Marlins, I said, "We'll take all 125 of them."

Another full page ad. But this time I was able to sell a brand new car for $1,699 and still make a good profit. It was my first — and last — run on Simcas. They were gone before I knew what happened.

Looking at it logically, it didn't make any sense trying to sell Marlins or Simcas. Even our salesmen were saying, "Bill, do you really think you can sell those things?"

But I had graduated from a course called "Faith 101" — and every principle was found in God's Word.

I learned that success does not come by falling at the feet of fear. It comes from standing tall on the "footings" of faith.

That is why I love that old song, "Only believe. Only believe. All things are possible. Only believe."

General Motors called me when they hit a brick wall with the roll-out of the diesel-engine Chevette. GM imported boatloads of diesel engines from Japan and placed them in an American made auto — allowing the car to get over 40 miles per gallon.

They shipped the cars to several dealerships — including mine — but sales were practically nil. We had two or three on our lot at the time. The problem was that the market was flooded with gasoline engines that had been converted to diesel, but they were not a *true* diesel — and people had nightmares with them.

Now came along a car with a pure diesel engine and nobody wanted to touch it. When GM called with their sales dilemma I said, "I'll buy every diesel-engine Chevette I can get my hands on." By this time other dealers were catching on and I could only get 150 of them.

My splashy ad said,

"CHEVETTE EQUIPPED WITH A SPECIAL JAPANESE ENGINE."

We sold out.

Just the other day I met a man who bought one of those cars years ago. He told me, "Bill, there's not enough money in the world to buy this little car from me. It's the best car I've ever had."

I made a lot of people happy — including me, since there was about $1,000 profit on every deal.

Predicaments and quandaries? Never. Life is too short for worry and fear. The world is filled with golden opportunities at every turn. Just begin to open your eyes to the possibilities.

When that opening comes, leap for it — with the boldness of a lion.

4

REPROGRAMMED BY THE "BIG THREE"

"Bill, you can't do that!"

"You'll never amount to anything."

Like a hammer hitting an anvil, those words were pounded into me as early as I can remember. I was programmed for failure.

The seeds of self-doubt had been planted so often and so deep that even when I was on the brink of success, I could not seem to take the final step. That's what happened in 1952 when I listened to my foreman at North American Aviation and closed my first venture into the used car business.

"Dream thieves" are everywhere — your neighbors, relatives, and fellow employees. They will use the most subtle means to sneak in and snatch your hope and vision. The title of Philadelphia entrepreneur Michael Cardone's book is true:

IT'S NEVER TOO LATE.

You can begin again.

What was the big difference between 1952 and 1957 in my two ventures into the second hand automobile business? The transformation was with *me* — not with the people around me. Most of my friends were saying, "Bill, you quit that kind of a business once before, what makes you think you can stay with it now?"

But this time was unlike anything my friends could imagine. I had been totally reprogrammed by the "Big Three." And I am not talking about GM, Ford, and Chrysler. My turn-around was a result of a total encounter with the Trinity — Father, Son, and Holy Ghost!

"I Believe in You"

For six years, since the moment I turned my life over to Christ, God was filling me with His Word and with His Spirit. It was not long until my mind-set of failure began to slowly dim and fade. In 1955, with a pastor who came to Columbus from Texas, we started a little church and I began to dig even deeper in the

Word.

In addition to reading God's principles for success, people were bringing me positive motivational material. Even before cassette tapes came along, an insurance salesman by the name of Glenn Erskine loaned me some 78 rpm records that made me want to go out and conquer the world. On those scratchy records I heard the voices of people like Earl Nightingale and Red Motley telling me I could be anything I would dare to believe.

Later, I got to know people like Dexter Yager and Don Held — men who had applied the principles of motivation to building empires in the Amway business. Their success and inspiration was like pouring fuel on a fire.

Was it possible? Could it be true? Did God really want to bless me beyond measure?

We've all heard the phrase, "Nothing succeeds like success." But the opposite is also just as true: "Nothing fails like failure." After the death of my father when I was just 19, it seemed that everything in my world just fell apart. Even after discovering that God loved me, it took a period of several years for my failure mentality to disappear.

I would look up and say, "Lord, how can you give me your best when you know how I was born, and how I have lived?" But day after day He began to water and nurture the seeds of greatness He had long before

41

planted inside me. He kept telling me, "Bill Swad, I believe in you. I have a great dream for your future."

Suddenly, I became plugged into the source. My energy and strength was not a Delco battery that would someday lose its voltage. What the Lord gave me was power and stamina that would last for a lifetime — and for eternity.

Great Expectations

My transformation from "stinkin' thinking" to Millionaire Mentality started with my heart, but soon affected every part of my being — my words, my actions, and my mind.

As a child, I had never been taught the importance of a healthy thought-life. No one took the time to tell me that a person becomes what he thinks about — or what he listens to and watches. But that is what scripture states. Paul instructed the church at Corinth: "For the weapons of our warfare are not carnal but mighty in God for pulling down strongholds, casting down arguments and every high thing that exalts itself against the knowledge of God, bringing every thought into captivity to the obedience of Christ . . ." (2 Corinthians 10:4,5)

Oh, the power of your thoughts. What you believe you will receive — whether it is good or bad. That is why our expectations are so vital.

Tell me you are going to go bankrupt and you may as well begin signing the papers. But tell me you are going to retire with a six-figure income and I'll be looking for you at St. Andrew's golf course in Boca Raton.

Someone once asked, "Bill, what if I don't get all that I expect?"

I told them,

"I'd rather receive five per cent of a great expectation than 100 per cent of nothing. Even if you shoot for the moon and miss, you're going to land among the stars."

That's not all bad.

The Lord knows that we are a reflection of what is happening on the inside. He said, "How can you, being evil, speak good things? For out of the abundance of the heart the mouth speaks." (Matthew 12:34) The change that took place in my heart affected my thoughts, and eventually impacted every word I spoke.

What can we do about negative thoughts? It takes a three step approach. One: recognize them for what they are. Two: destroy and eliminate them from your mind. Three: replace the thought with something positive.

I'll never forget telling a man about ten great businesses he could start with no money down. Within five minutes he had given me at least 20 excuses why they would not work for him. He didn't need an idea for an enterprise, he needed Norman Vincent Peale to immerse him in the river of positive thinking.

Why is our nation filled with more paupers than millionaires? This may sound simplistic, but it is true:

Far more people have a fear of loss than a desire for gain.

We are tempted every day to plant weeds of failure into seeds of greatness — not only in our personal life, but in the lives of those we influence. That is why it is vital that you are totally positive in your dealings with people. If you can't help someone, please don't hurt them. If you can't make them better, don't make them worse.

Coming from my background, developing a positive mental attitude was something that took years to achieve, but it was absolutely necessary.

What About Money?

The next great lesson was one I had a difficult time accepting — it was almost as if God had to pound it into my head.

I had to learn that money is not bad, it is good.

All my life I had been taught, "Well, money isn't everything." But the Bible taught me how important it truly is. "A feast is made for laughter, and wine makes merry; but money answers every thing." (Ecclesiastes 10:19)

Please don't misunderstand. I do not believe we should be obsessed with finances. But I have seen far more lives torn apart by oppression of poverty than by following God's rules regarding the use of wealth. I have been on both sides of the ledger and believe I know the realities involved.

Poverty does not belong in your life. The Bible says that, like sleep, "so shall your poverty come on you like a robber, and your need like an armed man." (Proverbs 6:11) In my Dake edition of the Bible it says, "Poverty will come with irresistible fury and you will not be prepared to cope with it."

Is money evil? Not at all. That is why Paul said to Timothy, "For the love of money is a root of all kinds of evil, for which some have strayed from the faith in their greediness, and pierced themselves through with many sorrows." (1 Timothy 6:10) There is a great difference between the *love* of money and the proper *use* of finances.

On your road to success, you can't take a detour every time someone accuses you of possessing wealth. You've worked for it, and it is a sign of God's favor. Having funds to sow into the soil of God's work is a blessing that cannot be measured.

No longer am I ashamed of talking about money. At our church, Christian Center in Columbus, we often say before the collection is taken on Sunday morning: "Hold up your tithes. Seed that toward a need in your life. You worked hard to earn that money, and the tithe belongs to the Lord. Now let's point that tithe toward a specific need." Oral Roberts made me aware of the importance of such an approach.

Wealthy Sinners?

I came to realize that God intends for His people to prosper, but what about the sinner? As I looked around, I saw many people who did not serve the Lord, and yet they seemed endowed with wealth. Did God have anything to say about that? He certainly did: "A good man leaves an inheritance to his children's children, but the wealth of the sinner is stored up for the righteous." (Proverbs 13:22)

When you fully comprehend the significance of that verse, you will realize that God intends for the wealth of the world to be yours.

More than once, I have had the treasure of an ungodly person transferred to my account.

"Mr. Swad, I'm in trouble with a 28 family apartment house," said the man on the other end of the phone. "You can buy it with almost no cash down and assume a 4.5% mortgage."

A short while after buying the units, the man called to say the arrangement had gone so well that he wanted me to take a 36-unit complex off his hands. Not only did I close the lucrative deal, but I was later able to leverage those apartment houses into my Chevrolet dealership.

Do I believe the wealth of the sinner is laid up for the just? Absolutely.

The dealership itself is the same story. Although the business was located in Columbus, the absentee owner lived in New York. He offered it to me at a very attractive price, and within the first three months I made more money than the $400,000 he lost in the previous year.

"I don't know why I sold this to you?" he told me a little later. Perhaps it was because I had the opportunity to tell the man about Jesus.

An unrepentant sinner may die with his wealth, and everything is gone. But those who know the Lord experience His blessing in this life, and the riches of the world to come.

You've Got a Counselor

It took the reprogramming of the Father, Son, and Holy Spirit to turn my life around. God the Father and God the Son are in heaven, but the Holy Spirit is here, now, to give you power to become everything God wants you to be.

Satan is stalking the land seeking whom he may devour, but there is a force much stronger that will open your eyes to truth and reveal what your future has in store.

If I asked you to spend an entire day with me, but never uttered one word, you would think I was rather strange. By five o'clock you'd be saying, "What are we doing? Can't you talk? Won't you give me a little attention?"

The Holy Spirit is just like that man. He is with you constantly, every moment of every day. But He never intrudes on your life — He only responds when you initiate the conversation. The Spirit, however, is grieved when we fail to invite Him to become a part of our life.

When I became conscious of the presence of the Spirit, it opened an entire new chapter in my relationship with God. Do you realize the Holy Spirit is with you while you are driving your car, eating your lunch, or mowing the lawn? He *never* leaves you. What is even more important is that He is your "counselor" and guide to teach you everything that was promised by the Father.

It matters not how bleak your background may have been. Every negative influence of your childhood can be totally transformed.

If it can happen to me, it can happen to you. Are you ready to be reprogrammed by the "Big Three?"

Checking out Martins Ferry, Ohio, at 14 months.

Plowing the farm as a teenager.

My $50 Ford at age 15.

Our little Holstein bull calf.

The birthplace of my father in Syria.

My aunt and uncle in Syria.

Our American Motors dealership became the nation's largest.

Signing the ABC-TV affiliate contract in Columbus for our daily Gospel music program sponsored by Bill Swad Motors.

Ohio governor James A. Rhoades, Bill Swad, Sr., and New York governor Nelson Rockefeller.

With Pat Robertson on the "700 Club" in 1974.

Ronald Reagan, Sally, and Bill.

Sharing the Word with "Papa Doc" Duvalier in Hati.

Our northern home in Columbus.

Our southern home in Boca Raton.

Bill and Sally.

Our Chevrolet dealership in Columbus today.

5

A PROMISE OF PROSPERITY

It is no fun living in poverty.

I found no joy in having to scrape together $5 or $10 a month to make a payment on a used refrigerator or washing machine. Even today, that is how millions of people live — not in some "third world" nation, but in the U.S.A.

When you are poor — and I have been there — it is almost impossible to conceive what it would be like to stay in a luxury hotel, drive an expensive car, or eat in a gourmet restaurant. Instead, you look at the rich with a combination of wonder, envy, and sometimes resentment.

Even after becoming a Christian, I joined a fellow-ship of believers who sincerely felt that wealthy people should be the objects of criticism, and I found myself saying, "Amen."

"Why is it," I thought as a young believer, "that the ungodly seemed to have all the wealth?" In the early 1950's, very few born again Christians could be counted in the higher income brackets. Our churches were small — and so was our thinking. Those who talked about "prosperity," or " affluence," had some-how crossed the line from being Godly to becoming "worldly."

The $1 Book

If being poor was being holy, I was ready for sainthood. To prove it, I was giving God nearly 15 cents out of the $1.47 I made every hour at the aircraft plant.

> *Then one day a man by the name of Oral Roberts came to Columbus. He pitched a huge tent that drew overflow crowds of up to 20,000.*

The impact on our city was beyond anything I had ever seen.

One evening, after the song service, they offered a book written by the evangelist. I was intrigued by the title:

GOD'S FORMULA FOR SUCCESS AND PROSPERITY.

Was it really possible that the Lord wanted us to succeed in business? I was anxious to find out and gave my $1 for the book. At home that night I could hardly fall asleep. I read with amazement the stories of people just like me — people that God had blessed beyond measure.

My eyes were opened to the fact that scripture — from Genesis to Revelation — was filled with the Lord's extraordinary promise of prosperity for the believer.

From that moment, my understanding of God's message of abundance seemed to explode. I began preaching the news to everyone who would listen — even before it was a popular thing to do.

Some have accused me of being an "Apostle of Prosperity." To me that is a cherished title because I believe God is trying to open the eyes of people who have been blinded by Satan regarding what is rightfully theirs. In recent years, millions of believers have become aware of what the Word really says about wealth and success.

Prosperity, I have discovered, is a relative term. To one person it is moving into a new one-bedroom apartment after living in a run-down shack. To another it might mean a three-car garage filled with a BMW, a Cadillac, and a Mercedes. But prosperity — *Biblical prosperity* — is simply the promise of God to pour out unlimited blessings on His people.

As Christians, you and I have entered into a contract with God. We have a "covenant" relationship. That's why we cannot compare the success of a non-believer with that of a follower of Christ — we're not covered by the same agreement and our lives are not guided by the same set of rules.

You may say, "But wait just a minute. This fellow started in business the same time I did, and he's doing so much better. They've got a new home, a new car, his kids are in a private college, and I'm barely making it."

But remember, you are playing by a different guidebook. He did not sign up to be in the same army as you. And as Yogi Berra said, "It's not over, 'til it's over!"

Three Reasons for Failure

I believe there are three important reasons some people in the body of Christ do not prosper. Let's examine them.

Reason number one: Ignorance regarding God's Laws.

"My people are destroyed for lack of knowledge. Because you have rejected knowledge, I also will reject you from being priest for Me; Because you have forgotten the law of your God, I also will forget your children." (Hosea 4:6)

Reason number two: Rebellion to the Word of God and what it teaches about prosperity.

What does scripture say about those who do not obey the commandments of the Lord? "And you shall grope at noonday, as a blind man gropes in darkness; you shall not prosper in your ways; you shall be only oppressed and plundered continually, and no one shall save you." (Deuteronomy 28:29)

But for the believer, He gave this promise: "And the Lord will make you the head and not the tail; you shall be above only, and not be beneath, if you heed the commandments of the Lord your God, which I command you today, and are careful to observe them." (v.13)

Reason number three: Covering sin rather than confessing it.

Proverbs 28:13 "He who covers his sins will not

prosper, but whoever confesses and forsakes them will have mercy." (Proverbs 28:13)

Do you want to know God's mercy? Begin confessing.

In my early years as a Christian I was taught that when the Bible talked about prosperity it was referring to the soul — not the savings account. The favorite illustration was the verse that read: "Beloved, I pray that you may prosper in all things and be in health, just as your soul prospers." (3 John 1:2)

Does that mean you have to live in an old house, drive a junk car and have five flat tires a week? "God does not want me to be rich," said one man, "He wants me to be humble." But I believe there is a difference between humility and stupidity. What does the Scripture really say? It says that

God wants you to prosper in <u>all</u> things — and that includes your health, your soul, and your money.

In the church I attended in 1952, there was a dear old man we called "Brother Trent" — he's gone on to be with the Lord now. He was upset because my shoes didn't have any holes in them. But his shoes were so dirty, I said, "Brother Trent, as a servant of the Lord I want to polish your shoes."

"Shine my shoes, "he retorted, "I *never* polish my

shoes. God wants me to be humble."

Perhaps I shouldn't have said it, but I told him, "That's not being humble, it's being filthy."

God was teaching me that if we are going to represent the King, we must present our best to Him — and to the world.

Goodbye to Guilt

I turned again to the words of Jesus: "The thief does not come except to steal, and to kill, and to destroy. I have come that they may have life, and that they may have it more abundantly." (John 10:10) Suddenly, what the Lord was saying became clear. Satan wants to steal my assets, kill my body, and destroy my soul. But Christ wanted to give me abundance in *all* things.

The more I studied the Word the bolder I became. One day I stood up and said, "Devil! Stop trying to place a guilt trip on me about money. God told me that the riches of the world are mine, and I am claiming them!"

The Bible does not say that you will suddenly discover instant success — it's not like striking oil in Alaska. But by following His precepts, your time of harvest will surely come. The Apostle Paul said, "And let us not grow weary while doing good, for in due season we shall reap if we do not lose heart." (Galatians 6:9)

I have counseled with hundreds of people over the

years. And far too often the sessions were triggered by the fact that someone's house or car was being repossessed because of lack of finances.

You may ask, "Is being poor really that destructive?" Here is what the Bible says: "The rich man's wealth is his strong city; the destruction of the poor is their poverty." (Proverbs 10:15)

Perhaps the real reason the message of prosperity was turned off by the church earlier in this century is because they saw damage being done by people who were thriving. Let me give you an example.

Let's say that you started a small enterprise and became very prosperous. A short time later you receive a call from your pastor saying: "We've missed you in church for the last few weeks. Where have you folks been?"

You respond, "Well, pastor, God has been blessing our business so much that we have to work every Sunday just to keep up with it all." Then you add, "But don't worry, we still love the church and will be sending our tithes."

Friend, the Lord is not really interested in your money without <u>*you.*</u> *He wants both.*

Don't let your success become a substitute for a personal relationship with the Almighty. If you aren't careful, you're life will become what Solomon described: "The rich man's wealth is his strong city, and like a high wall in his own esteem. Before destruction the heart of a man is haughty, and before honor is humility." (Proverbs 18:11,12)

Some may complain, "Is money all you ever talk about around here?" I have found that in a church, the person who whines the most about the mention of money is a person who is not a strong giver — and as a result, has few blessings.

Scripture, however, gives distinct and strong counsel about your use of finances. ". . . then you say in your heart, 'My power and the might of my hand have gained me this wealth.' And you shall remember the Lord your God, for it is He who gives you power to get wealth, that He may establish His covenant which He swore to your fathers, as it is this day." (Deuteronomy 8:17,18)

Forgetting the Source

Why am I involved in the work of a local church instead of wasting my Sundays on a golf course or at a beach? It is because of the opportunity to mend the lives of broken people. But that takes money — for bricks and mortar, for lights, and for an outreach to a community that is hurting.

One of the great lessons I learned was that money is our friend, not our enemy. And *people* with money are our friends, not our enemies.

So often, I have been asked, "Bill, why are there so few people who have experienced success — like yourself — who will spend their time teaching what God has to say about prosperity?" My answer is, "They're out there, but they have left the church." They have deserted the body of Christ and become self-centered and self-satisfied. They forgot the source of their success.

God has such great things planned for you. "Now it shall come to pass, if you diligently obey the voice of the Lord your God, to observe carefully all His commandments which I command you today, that the Lord your God will set you high above all nations of the earth. And all these blessings shall come upon you and overtake you, because you obey the voice of the Lord your God." (Deuteronomy 28:1-2)

"And the Lord will grant you plenty of goods, in the fruit of your body, in the increase of your livestock, and in the produce of your ground, in the land of which the Lord swore to your fathers to give you." (Deuteronomy 28:11)

But here is the Lord's warning: "When you have eaten and are full, then you shall bless the Lord your God for the good land which He has given you. Beware that you do not forget the Lord your God by not keeping His commandments, His judgments, and His statutes which I command you today . . ." (Deuteronomy 8:10,11)

Your New Account

Without question it was the Lord that caused my business to prosper and I made a life-long commitment to share His goodness with every fiber of my being. But it goes much deeper than my knowledge and experience with finance.

> *I believe that money is of God —*
> *and that it is <u>ours.</u> The same Lord*
> *that owns the cattle on a thousand hills*
> *has opened an account in your name.*

What has He prepared for you? The Bible says that the New Jerusalem is going to have streets of gold. Can you imagine? We get a small piece of gold and wear it thinking, "Wow, this is great." But someday soon you are going to *walk* on it!

If you plan to enter that Heavenly City, never forget your promises to the Lord. Whether your business is a pizza shop, or a real estate business, or whatever, dedicate it to God. Say, "Father, no matter how big it gets or how prosperous, I'm going to remember the body of Christ and the work of the Lord. Jesus, I'll never, never forget you."

If God says, "I'm going to give you power to get wealth," that is exactly what He will do. And if the Lord had a contract, or covenant with the Old Testament people, He has a covenant with you. The more you study scripture, the clearer it becomes. He planted the seeds of greatness within you and provides the dynamic energy to make them grow.

The Apostle Paul tells you, ". . . my God shall supply all your need according to His riches in glory by Christ Jesus." (Philippians 4:19

The Lord keeps His covenants — and that includes His promise of prosperity.

6

THE $100 DILEMMA

Just after launching my business enterprise in 1957, I found myself totally broke — not even enough cash to buy a sandwich.

It was 7:00 p.m. and I didn't know what to do. Evangelist Rex Humbard's brother, Clem, had come to town and our little church along with one other small "Foursquare" congregation put up a tent and sponsored his revival meeting.

My promise was that I would close the car lot every night at 7:30 p.m. and rush over to the tent. That was a real sacrifice, especially since I was just starting my business.

Running out of cash was not something I had expected. In the first four days of my used car business I made more money than in any *month* of my life. After selling four or five cars, I thought, "This is better than I ever imagined!" My overhead was low, the cash profits were great, and I had not hired any help.

That afternoon, however, when I stopped by the bank to deposit some checks to cover the purchases of some other cars,

I looked at the balance in the account and was shocked. There wasn't a penny to spare.

So I was standing on the lot that evening with absolutely no money in my pocket.

I did have something of value, however. I had an account full of faith.

"At Least One Dollar"

As I paced back and forth across the lot I thought, "Now, Lord, you know I need to put something in the offering tonight at the revival when the plate is passed." I hated the thought of being a sponsor of the meeting and having nothing to contribute. Even if I had just a quarter, I could hold it tight in my hand and drop it down in the plate — no one would know what it was. But I didn't even have a nickel.

"Lord," I said, "Please let me put at least a dollar in the collection tonight."

At that moment a car drove onto the lot. I thought, "Thank you, Jesus. This is it!" I recognized the man. He was a construction worker building houses in the neighborhood.

"Look, I want a piece-of-junk car that I can drive into the fields and around a building site," he told me.

"Herman, I've got the perfect car for you," I replied. "I just took in this 1952 Plymouth that has been a local taxicab. This car knows every street in Columbus. It will take you any place you want to go, because it's got about 400,000 miles on it."

Then I told him, "I want about $150 for it, because the guy who traded it just put in a new motor. It doesn't look like much, but it runs great."

"That's what I need," he said. "I want to be able to drive into the mud. Plus, my foremen need to haul a lot of building materials in it. It looks like the right car for me." Then he added, "But I'm not going to give you but $100."

He opened his billfold and I couldn't help but notice that he had a $100 bill and a couple of ones. Instantly I had it all figured out. I thought, "If I can get a hundred and one, tomorrow I can take the hundred bucks down to the Ford dealer and I can pick up a pretty nice car — or maybe even two not-so-nice ones. I'll clean them up and sell them for maybe $300 each. And I can put the dollar in the offering."

So I argued with him for about ten minutes. I said "Look, Herman, I've got to have at least $102."

He shook his head saying, "All I have is $102. I've got to put a couple of dollars worth of gas in it."

My final offer was: "Give me $101 and put a dollars worth of gas in the car."

He agreed and gave me the $100 bill and the extra dollar. At that point in my life I had never personally held a $100 dollar bill, and I was excited about what had just happened.

Ready For the Offering

The music had already started when I arrived at the little tent. Clem was singing, his wife Priscilla was playing the harp, and I was ready for the offering. I put the dollar in my left pocket so I wouldn't make a mistake.

Clem Humbard walked up to the microphone and said, "Friends, I was praying this afternoon and the Holy Spirit impressed upon me that I am not supposed to take up an offering tonight."

I thought, "Praise God! Now I've got the dollar I can put in *tomorrow* night."

The evangelist continued, "When I was praying I saw a vision. I saw three people under this tent tonight with a $100 bill in their pocket. If you will just stand up and come forward I'll tell you what else God has shown me." Two ladies stood up and walked toward the platform.

As they walked, I looked around to see who the third person would be. It certainly was getting hot under that tent. Or was it just the dilemma I faced?

I had never given $100 in an offering before, because I didn't have the $100 to give. Was God testing me? The money hadn't been in my pocket for more than 30 minutes and I was just getting used to the feel of it — but I knew what I had to do. I walked to the front.

Humbard anointed each of us as he spoke a word from the Lord. He said, "By noon tomorrow each of you will be blessed seven fold."

When the clock struck 12 the next day I had sold three cars and made over $1000.

You can imagine what that did to my young faith.

God opened the windows of blessing and He has never closed them until this day.

Giving Before Getting?

Jesus told His followers, "But seek first the kingdom of God and His righteousness, and all these things shall be added to you." (Matthew 6:33)

As a new Christian I asked, "What things?" They told me "spiritual things."

I said, "Wait a minute. What if I get all these

71

spiritual things and the Sheriff evicts me and puts my furniture on the curb? Would God be pleased? Surely He has some other things in mind."

Then I read the scripture, "Give, and it will be given to you: good measure, pressed down, shaken together, and running over . . ." (Luke 6:38)

I thought, "How can I give before I get?" And God said, "That's not the way it is, son. You've got to give first." I learned there is *always* something we can present to the Lord. Even if you are totally broke, you have your time and your talent. Begin to sow seeds. What Jesus really said was that your giving actually causes God to act. In school I was taught the law of physics that says: *for every action there is a reaction.* But God established that principle long before science.

When I was an agnostic as a teenager, I attended an atheist church. The pastor and I were good friends — we used to get drunk together. There was one principle, however, that he taught us — tithing. They were so strict on the topic that they checked up on us to see that we were obeying. Ten dollars of every $100 I received each month from milking cows went to that so-called church.

I had no idea what the Bible said concerning the subject. I did not know that the tithe belongs to God — because I didn't believe there *was* a God.

Later, when I learned God's plan for success, tithing became more than a law of the Kingdom. It became an indispensable part of my life. If you were to ask me, "Bill, what has been the greatest contributing factor to your Millionaire Mentality?" Without question I would tell you it is the principle of tithing.

A Thief is a Thief

You may say, "With all the money you have made, it's easy for you to tithe." No.

If a man will steal from God when he is making a hundred dollars a week, he'll steal from God when he's making a million dollars a week.

Because he is a thief.

A recent survey indicates that 82% percent of people who call themselves Christians are stealing from God. They are not tithers. "Stealing?" you may ask. What does the Bible say? "Will a man rob God? Yet you have robbed Me! But you say, 'In what way have we robbed You?' In tithes and offerings." (Malachi 3:8)

After the Lord says, "Bring all the tithes into the storehouse, " (v.10) He promises to "rebuke the devourer for your sakes . . ." (v.11) Who is stealing your money? Satan. By failing to obey the Lord, you become as "he who earns wages . . . to put into a bag with holes." (Haggai 1:6)

It's a message that is proclaimed in far too few

churches. Let's face it, it's difficult to preach tithing to a congregation filled with people wearing stolen shoes, stolen jewelry, and driving stolen cars. That may sound harsh, but the non-tither is stealing from the Lord and spending the money on himself.

You ask, "Are you really that fanatical about tithing?" I am totally convinced that none of the success principles I am telling you about will fully work without it.

"But we have a New Testament church," you may say. "We're living under grace, not law."

My friend, Jesus talked about the subject. He discussed it because the Pharisees were only tithing, and not presenting a balanced life to God. "Woe to you, scribes and Pharisees, hypocrites! For you pay tithe of mint and anise and cumin, and have neglected the weightier matters of the law: justice and mercy and faith. These you ought to have done, without leaving the others undone." (Matthew 23:23) What did He want them to do? *All* of it — including tithing.

Paul told the church at Corinth, "Now concerning the collection for the saints, as I have given orders to the churches of Galatia, so you must do also: On the first day of the week let each one of you lay something aside, storing up as he may prosper . . ." (1 Corinthians 16:1,2)

The principle of the Word of God is the giving of the tenth. As my friend Oral Roberts says,

"You don't pay your tithe. You bring your tithe."

It is not yours, it's God's.

Assets or Liabilities?

There are two major forces in this world — the power of God and the power of Satan. The devil wants the sinner down the street from you to prosper, because that money won't be used for the Lord. Satan delights in convincing you that you can't afford to be a tither.

A lady in our church once told me, "There's a poor family in our neighborhood and we use our tithe money to feed them."

"You're absolutely wrong, I told her." God commands that we bring it into the "storehouse." Because of faithful giving, our church has been able to build a "love center" that has fed and clothed over 2,000 families a year.

If you want to be blessed of God, sit down with your family and say, "We are going to make a commitment to the Lord to bring our tithe to the church every week." Despite your present circumstances, make a total declaration that you are going to bring to the Lord what is rightfully His.

Those funds are not for car payments or a new wardrobe — they're God's.

Because of the Lord's blessing, my wife and I can

give not only our tithe — but much more. Recently, after a large real estate transaction, we were able to give 150% or our annual income. My accountant just scratched his head.

Visiting with my friends Sam and Bette Rudd, Sam told me,

"Bill, every asset that we have on earth will become a liability in heaven. "

That's why I'm sending my investment ahead.

The Lord said to bring *all* the tithe. Not 4% or ever 9%. — that's not a tithe. But when you present your *increase* to Him, He will "open for you the windows of heaven and pour out for you such blessing that there will not be room enough to receive it." (Malachi 3:10)

The sale of a battered taxi for $100 was of minor consequence. But think what I'd have missed had I kept the money in my pocket.

7

THE BALANCING ACT

As a kid, I remember going to the Fenray movie theater in Martins Ferry. I was especially thrilled when they showed films of a circus — I had never seen one in person. The trained elephants and juggling acts were great, but I was fascinated most by the daring man who could gingerly walk across a tight-rope by balancing a large pole in his hand.

After building and operating five successful new car dealerships in Columbus, I felt like the man on that rope. Life had become a balancing act — and was about to tilt in the wrong direction.

There was no question about it. The five dealerships could easily have become ten. Offers and opportunities were coming in from all sides. "Bill, there's a Buick dealership available in Indiana." "Would you like to have a Honda franchise near Cincinnati?" If I chose the path of explosive growth, I could have easily built a national conglomerate of 100 dealerships. The pattern of success we had established could be duplicated again and again. Should I become a "McSwad's"?

"A Truckload of Cash"

I had to face some serious questions.

Was I willing to sell out my life for money? What about my commitment to serve the Lord — and His people?

The decision wasn't made in a mahogany-paneled corporate boardroom. It was made on my knees at a simple altar of prayer. I promised God I would simplify my life by operating one large dealership, and give Him half of my time and my finances. One by one, we sold the dealerships for more than healthy profits.

By now you know that I did not build a business empire by accidentally finding a truckload of cash. I started with a simple partnership — just me and the Lord — and I worked, and worked, and worked.

Some people come into a relationship with the Lord saying, "God, what can you do for me?" Or, if they think they can make it on their own, say, "Lord, if I ever need you I'll be sure to call."

My connection to the Creator was totally different. I had a twenty-four-hour-a-day, seven-day-a-week alliance with God that was extremely serious. I knew from the beginning that I was not playing church. God was right by my side and had a dramatic impact on every move I made.

Was I ever discouraged? Of course, but never with God — it was always with people.

An Unexpected Answer

In 1965, after building a new church in Columbus, I discovered that many people in the body of Christ did not recognize Jesus as Lord. I wondered, "Why are these people back-biting, criticizing, and hurting each other so?"

Frankly, I became disgusted with what I saw and told the Lord, "I want out." It reached the point where I thought, "Do I really need all this? Wouldn't I be better off putting both feet in the business world making millions more?" I longed to serve Jesus and be close to Him, but wanted to be far away from fighting Christians that seemed filled with conflict and hate.

Wasn't life supposed to be tranquil and serene serving the Lord?

On a Saturday night I went to my "prayer closet." Actually it was a narrow space under the basement stairs. I liked it because I could tuck myself in really tight where the steps came down to the floor — I felt "locked in" with the Lord.

For more than two hours I wept and prayed, asking, "Jesus, what is wrong with the body of Christ?"

Then the answer came. But it was not what I expected. The Lord clearly told me, "Bill, you are part of the problem because you do not show enough love." He convicted me for not being tender and compassionate toward the people who had a spirit of enmity and malice.

> *Then, in an instant, God*
> *showed me an amazing vision.*
> *It was unlike anything*
> *that had happened to me.*

He told me to stand before the congregation the next morning and reveal everything He had shown.

The next morning I was in a quandary. I didn't have a message to preach since I had been so upset at the behavior within the church. Then I was convicted regarding my own lack of love. And now the Lord wanted me to share a specific prophetic vision that was about to happen.

As I walked up to the pulpit, the peace of God came over me like warm oil being poured from heaven. And He gave me the courage to share the revelation.

"Be sure you are here for the service tonight. We

are going to witness one of the greatest miracles you have ever seen," I told the congregation. "Last night as I was praying, God gave me a vision and told me to reveal it to you."

The room became totally quiet as I said, "The Lord showed me the faces of three people that I have never seen before. I have no idea who they are. But tonight, they are going to be sitting four pews from the back on the left side. So this evening, when you come to church, leave that pew empty."

Then I said, "God told me that one of the women has cancer and she will be healed." The vision was so clear that I told them, "One of the ladies has reddish hair, one is blond, and the other has black hair." I told them the exact location where the sick person would be sitting.

That very moment, a wave of expectation and love swept over the church. I chose as my text, "Is anyone among you sick? Let him call for the elders of the church, and let them pray over him, anointing him with oil in the name of the Lord. And the prayer of faith will save the sick, and the Lord will raise him up. And if he has committed sins, he will be forgiven." (James 5:14,15)

As the Lord began to heal the physical needs of the church, you could sense a healing of forgiveness taking place among the members. Without question, the transformation of love that had taken place within me was contagious.

81

The Empty Pew

That night, I couldn't wait to get to church. The service started at 7:30 p.m. and all eyes were on that empty pew. During the song service, every time the back door opened it seemed that the entire congregation turned around to see who it was.

At 8:00 p.m. I was whispering to the song leader, "Go ahead and sing another one."

I thought, "Lord, did you give me a vision, or was I dreaming?" Would I be embarrassed because I had told the church something that would not happen? Yet it was the strongest prophesy I had ever received from God.

By 8:15 p.m. it seemed we had sung every chorus the piano player knew — and I was beginning to sweat.

Not knowing what to do, I read the exact same passage from James I had used that morning. "Is anyone among you sick? Let him call for the elders of the church . . ."

As I was reading, I looked up and saw three women walking down the aisle — a blond, a redhead, and a lady with dark black hair. No one told them where to find a seat. They walked to the fourth pew from the back on the left.

Like electricity, the power of God was bouncing off the walls of that sanctuary.

"Ladies," I said, "before you are even seated just come on down here. I want to pray for you."

As the three of them stood before me at the altar, I said to the woman in the middle, "I had a vision of you last night." She looked stunned. And I told her, "Don't be alarmed, but I saw trees growing inside you — like cancer spreading in your body. How long do you have to live?"

Her voice quivering, she said, "The doctors told me less than six months." The entire church began to believe God for a miracle.

That happened several years ago and the woman is still alive today.

The church was transformed — and so was I — when we realized that God's blessing was greater than our bickering. His great purpose was greater than our problems.

Noah Said It

There is no way I could enjoy Millionaire Mentality without receiving a baptism of love. It adds a dimension to life that no amount of money can buy. As I tell people, "We have no choice — we're in this thing together."

When Noah put all those animals in the ark I believe he said, "Now foxes, you can't eat those rabbits because we only have two." And he probably told the elephant, "Don't step on the cat."

What is the greatest commandment? Jesus summed

it up when He said, "A new commandment I give to you, that you love one another; as I have loved you . . ." (John 13:34) That means forgiveness -- no jealousy, no hatred. If you want your life to prosper you have to bury greed and guilt.

Aren't you glad that love and guilt cannot coexist? When you accept one, you deny the other. Perhaps there have been times when you were overcome by remorse and regret because of some act. You may have felt that what you did was so wrong that it could never be healed.

Remember this: God has the ability and the desire to forgive the vilest sinner. The Prodigal Son found himself in the pigpen of life. But he made a conscious decision. He said, "I will go back to my father's house, because he loves me and holds no grievances."

Our Heavenly Father reacts in exactly the same way. He holds no grudges against you for what may have happened yesterday. Before we can be motivated to be successful at life, the inner man must be healed.

> *When the hurts of the past*
> *have been released, you are*
> *suddenly free to reach the*
> *potential God has planned.*

Every adverse thing that has ever happened to you needs to be released and given to the Lord, so that you never have the burden of it again. God wants you to be happy with *you!*

The Bible says, "And you shall love the Lord your God with all your heart, with all your soul, with all your mind, and with all your strength. This is the first commandment. And the second, like it, is this: You shall love your neighbor as yourself. There is no other commandment greater than these." (Mark 12:30-31)

A New Perspective

Do you really want the capacity to love your neighbor? It begins within your heart — only when it is clean and pure can you truly love yourself.

If your desire is to be at peace with God, you need to live in harmony with those around you. Don't try to reach the top by stepping on people you despise. That's a short path to failure. It is important to know that the same Father that loves you, also loves them.

God wants to transform your mentality, but first He must change your heart. If you have never asked Christ to forgive you of your sins, take a moment right now to ask Him to become your Lord and Savior. "For God so loved the world that He gave His only begotten Son, that whoever believes in Him should not perish but have everlasting life." (John 3:16)

Are you ready for a balanced life? It begins with a heart of love that only Christ can give. The Lord will provide the stability you need to keep every area of your life in proper perspective — your family, your career, your finances, and your faith.

It doesn't matter how far the
tight-rope is stretched, or how
far above the ground you may be.
With the Lord providing the balance,
you'll make it to the other side.

8

FLYING HIGH

Last week I rushed out to Port Columbus International Airport for a flight to Florida. As my car drove into the area where the private planes are parked, I couldn't help but look across the field — there was the North American aviation plant where I had worked for $1.47 an hour.

It was only a few hundred yards away, but it seemed like a million miles. It was in that factory that I first fell in love with aircraft and dreamed about flying. Now, instead of constructing planes, I was collecting them.

Ahead of me was my Cessna 182. I call it my "little buddy" since we go so many places together. It's loaded with the latest technical equipment — carries eight hours worth of fuel and can cruise at 13,000 feet. It was previously owned by Tom Landry, former coach of the Dallas Cowboys.

Down the line was our twin-engine Cessna 421. Then there was our Citation jet that we lease out through a fixed-base operator, but can use whenever we want.

As we taxied down the runway I pulled the control wheel for lift-off. Within a few short minutes we were flying high — the visibility was clear, the clouds were scattered, and there was no turbulence.

What did it take to rise from the assembly line to the blue skies? It took the belief in a flight plan that I had filed many, many years before.

Your future will not happen by accident. Far too often I have heard people say, "If God wants me to be successful, I'll be successful." They place the entire burden of their life on the Almighty and fold their arms waiting for something great and unexpected to take place.

Three Vital Laws

You need to know that there are specific laws that govern your future. It is only when those laws are *obeyed* that your goals can be achieved. Here are the three fundamental laws I had to learn.

Number 1: GOD'S LAW.

The Lord is in the blessing business, but only for

those who live according to the rules He has established. Look closely at His precepts and requirements: *For every blessing, there is a condition that must be met.*

"He who sows sparingly will also reap sparingly, and he who sows bountifully will also reap bountifully." (2 Corinthians 9:6)

"Give, and it will be given to you . . ." (Luke 6:38)

"For everyone who asks receives, and he who seeks finds, and to him who knocks it will be opened." (Matthew 7:8)

"No good thing will He withhold from those who walk uprightly." (Psalms 84:11)

Do you notice the pattern? God's indisputable laws require action on your part. "If they obey and serve Him, they shall spend their days in prosperity, and their years in pleasures." (Job 36:11) His outpouring *follows* obedience.

Number 2: MAN'S LAW.

"Why did the devil take her life?" a friend cried at the funeral parlor.

The lady was a God-fearing Christian who paid her tithes, never missed a church service, and was a servant to all who were in need. But on her way home from church she drove through a stop sign and was instantly killed in a head-on collision.

"The devil didn't take her life," I explained. "She

disobeyed the laws of man." Nowhere in scripture can you find protection for a person who violates the ordinances of government.

A very dear friend received the message one day that his beautiful daughter and her husband had been killed in a plane crash. Since he deeply loved the Lord, some questioned why God would allow such a tragedy to happen.

But wait a minute. The laws of man had been violated. The pilot was not qualified to fly the multi-engine airplane, and the airplane had not passed the proper annual inspections to fly. When I read the FAA report on that accident, I shook my head in disbelief. The laws of aviation had been transgressed.

As a pilot, I live by faith and fly by faith — but the airplane doesn't rely on my belief. I have to obey the laws of man.

Number 3: NATURAL LAW.

I vividly remember the Sunday an evangelist from California spoke in our church. The next morning, my wife Sally and I had breakfast with him before he returned to the west coast.

"Can I give you a little advice?" I said. "You shouldn't be flying around the Sierra Nevada mountains in that Cessna 310. Those peaks are too high — you've really got to watch it."

I knew that just one flight with heavy cargo could put him in danger. Four days later I received a phone call: his plane had just crashed and the evangelist had been killed. He flew into the side of a mountain and the mountain won.

Friend, you cannot violate natural laws. Don't expect divine intervention when you have disobeyed the rules of physics and gravity.

What did the great prophet Hosea say? "My people are destroyed for lack of knowledge." (Hosea 4:6)

As I told a friend, "Faith is the substance of things hoped for the evidence of things not seen, but if you pull up on the train tracks and there is a diesel coming, you're going to be seeing Jesus real soon."

What does the song say? "Trust and obey, for there's no other way." You have an obligation to observe natural laws.

If you're a smoker and die of lung cancer — or you're grossly overweight and neglect the laws of health, don't blame either God or the devil for taking your life. You have the responsibility to heed the rules of nature.

It Wouldn't Stop!

When I began to practice God's divine principles in my life and in my business, it was like a flood of blessing that I couldn't contain. If I tried to shut the front door, it would come in through the back. If I tried to close the window, He'd pour it through the roof. The blessings wouldn't stop.

91

The land and building where we started an American Motors Company dealership in 1962 is still ours. When we sold the franchise in 1975, the new owners leased the land for 25 years — and now our checks come from the Chrysler Corporation.

When we bought the land for our Chrysler/Plymouth dealership, it was nothing more than an alley on a little two lane road — there were not even sidewalks. I believe the Lord knew that within two years it would be one of the most important North-South corridors in our city. We had 650 feet of frontage. When we sold that dealership in 1978 it had become one of the top four in the U.S. and provided me with income many, many years later.

We relocated our Datsun dealership that had been in a ghetto, to a building with a $2 million mortgage. We bought it at a sheriff's sale for $890,000 — the entire property. We sold the business a few years later for more than $3 million.

So often I stand on the very spot where a string of lights and the little office shack stood on our original car lot in 1957. Today I am in our showroom, a giant 60,000 square foot Chevrolet dealership where our son, Bill, Jr., is Vice President and part owner. It has expanded to 19 acres — a truck and van center across the street, and a shopping center next door.

When I review our balance sheet of assets and liabilities, I realize that property and possessions are only a means to an end. The only things that really matter are the deposits in my heavenly account.

Forget About Yesterday

You might be thinking, "It's too late for me to attempt success." You know, I thought that when I was just 27 years old. But age is not significant. I remember telling Colonel Sanders about Jesus on a flight from Toronto to Columbus just before his conversion experience. He was 65 when he began Kentucky Fried Chicken.

Ray Kroc started McDonald's when he was in his fifties. It's never too late.

Just as important is that you forget the shortcomings of your past. Education and experience are wonderful, but you can make up for your lack of these in a big hurry.

Every time the devil comes against you and tells you about your past, why don't you tell him about his future — it is doomed for destruction.

Then you can go on to greater things.

If the failure syndrome I knew as a child could be replaced by a dream of success, anything is possible. No one told me about God — much less about His plan for prosperity. But all of that changed.

Let's say you've made some miserable mistakes along the way. Don't count on your friends to encourage you to start over. They'll most likely say, "I know

93

someone else that had the same problem and they never did make it." Instead believe the words of Richard Roberts' book, *God of the Second Chance.* You can begin again.

No matter how many failures you've had, there is hope. Satan will come along and try to wipe you out by whispering, "You're not smart enough to start over."

The seeds of greatness God has planted in you are crying out to grow — they just need to be nurtured.

Dr. Robert Schuller said, "Let God turn your scars into stars." That is not easy. But the Lord can transform your stumbling blocks into stepping stones.

You say, "But my tragedy was bigger than yours." The size of the adversity is meaningless to the Lord. He can cure a simple headache or rescue a business from bankruptcy. Whether it is the healing of your memories or solving your money problems, He can turn every unsightly scar into a brilliant star. And every stepping stone will be placed a little bit higher.

Perhaps you have been through divorce, remarried and someone told you that you're on your way to hell. Remember, God is love. He loved you before, He loves you now, and He will love you in the future. The Lord's desire is to see you elevated above your problems.

Higher Than You've Ever Been

You must come to the realization that, "Yes, there are seeds of greatness in me!" You may have an empty checkbook and your business may be hanging by a thread. Step back a few paces and take a new look at your possibilities.

Right now, invite the Lord to become your business partner and watch what begins to happen. He will give you greater dreams than you ever imagined. And He'll keep you on course to see them come to pass. I know! It happened to me.

From the poverty of Martins Ferry to a Citation jet was an adventure I would never exchange. To escape from hand-me-down clothes and "holey" shoes to being able to give over $2 million to God's work took a change of heart and a change of mind.

Millionaire Mentality did not come overnight. It was the result of heartache, prayer, diligence, belief, and — above all — the application of the principles of God's Word.

If I did not believe the same thing can happen to you, I would close my Bible and place a padlock on the doors of our church.

Fasten your seat belt! I believe you are about to fly — higher than you've ever been before.

95

Write for a
complete list of
INSPIRATIONAL AND MOTIVATIONAL MATERIALS
by Bill Swad, Sr.

BOOKS
AUDIO CASSETTES
VIDEO CASSETTES
TRAINING MATERIALS
STUDY GUIDES

Bill Swad, Sr.
c/o Christian Center
298 South Rocky Fork Drive
Gahanna, Ohio 43230